big
NATE
OUT LOUD

big
NATE
OUT LOUD

by LINCOLN PEIRCE

SCHOLASTIC INC.
New York Toronto London Auckland
Sydney Mexico City New Delhi Hong Kong

ISBN 978-0-545-42702-9

12 11 10 9 8 7 6 5 4 3 2   11 12 13 14 15 16/0

Printed in the U.S.A.   23

First Scholastic printing, November 2011

These strips appeared in newspapers from April 2, 2007, through November 4, 2007.

For the Rhode Islanders

WHAT THE...?

WHAT IS **THAT**?

IT'S A SOMBRERO, AMIGOS!

4/5

SOON EVERYBODY WILL COPY ME BY GETTING THEIR **OWN** SOMBREROS! IT'LL BE SOMBRERO MANIA! AND IT ALL STARTED WITH **ME**!

HEAR THAT, MARCUS? YOU'RE NOT THE **ONLY** TREND-SETTER AROUND!

YES HE IS!

NOW **THAT'S** A TREND I COULD GET BEHIND!

Peirce

I LOVE THIS TIME OF YEAR! IT'S JOB-FREE!

JOB-FREE?

NO RESPONSIBILITIES, TEDDY!

THE SNOW HAS MELTED, SO THERE'S NOTHING TO SHOVEL...

THE GRASS HASN'T STARTED GROWING YET, SO THERE'S NOTHING TO **MOW**...

...AND THERE AREN'T ANY **LEAVES** ON THE GROUND, SO THERE'S NOTHING TO **RAKE**!

NO RESPONSIBILITIES! JOB-FREE!

WHAT A REVOLTING TURN OF EVENTS.

DANG IT!

© 2007 by NEA, Inc.

4/13

WHAT'S UP, PEST?

THERE'S NOBODY TO PLAY CATCH WITH.

FRANCIS HAS A SWIM MEET... TEDDY IS VISITING HIS GRAND-PARENTS... NOBODY ELSE IS AROUND!

WHAT ABOUT DAD?

DAD?

SURE, ISN'T HE ALWAYS BUGGING YOU TO PLAY CATCH?

HE'D PROBABLY LOVE IT IF **YOU** ASKED **HIM** FOR A CHANGE!

HMM...

YOU'RE RIGHT, ELLEN! I'LL GIVE HIM ONE OF THOSE FATHER-SON MOMENTS AND TOTALLY MAKE HIS DAY!

DAD! HEY, DAD! WANNA HUCK A BALL AROUND?

I'M TRYING TO DO MY TAXES!

WANNA PLAY CATCH?

MRS. GODFREY, I FOUND MY HOME-WORK IN MY DESK! I **TOLD** YOU I'D DONE IT!

WHOOPS, WAIT A SEC. THERE'S SOMETHING STUCK TO IT.

PIK PIK

NIBBLE NIBBLE MUNCH MUNCH CRUNCH

IT'S EITHER TOMATO SAUCE OR SOME KIND OF PUDDING.

OOLP!

NATE, THROW THIS GARBAGE AWAY.

GARBAGE? THERE'S LOTS OF GOOD STUFF IN HERE!

WELL, I SAY IT'S GARBAGE!

...AND I SAY IT HAS VALUE!

SO IF I GRAB SOMETHING AT **RANDOM** FROM THIS MESS, YOU CLAIM IT WILL SOMEHOW BE **WORTH** SOMETHING?

ABSOLUTELY!

ZW!P!

"A PRIEST, A RABBI, AND A DUCK WALK INTO A BAR..."

OH! THAT ONE'S **PRICE**LESS!

CHESTER: PITCHING...
FRANCIS: CATCHING...
TEDDY: CENTER FIELD...
NATE: RIGHT FIELD...

AGAIN?

WELL, WHY NOT? YOU'RE A VERY GOOD RIGHT FIELDER!

YEAH, BUT...

NOTHING EVER **HAPPENS** OUT THERE!

THAT'S JUST THE WAY BASEBALL IS, NATE. SOMETIMES THEY HIT IT TO YOU, AND SOME- TIMES THEY DON'T!

YEAH, I KNOW...

...BUT IT'S JUST SO **BORING** STANDING AROUND FOR NINE INNINGS!

JUST GET OUT THERE, NATE. I'M SURE YOU'LL FIND **SOME** WAY TO KEEP YOURSELF AMUSED.

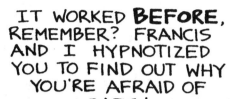

© 2007 by NEA, Inc.

HERE'S MY HOMEWORK, MRS. GODFREY! YOU WANT **NEAT**? YOU'VE **GOT** NEAT!

NO RIPS, NO WRINKLES, NO SMUDGES, NO STAINS! ABSOLUTELY NO MISTAKES OF ANY KIND!

5/1

YOU WERE SUPPOSED TO ANSWER THE TEN QUESTIONS AT THE END OF CHAPTER TWO, NOT THE TWO QUESTIONS AT THE END OF CHAPTER TEN.

© 2007 by NEA, Inc.

OKAY, ONE TEENSY LITTLE MISTAKE.

TRY AGAIN.

JENNY, M'LADY! WHAT DO YOU THINK OF THE NEW ME?

WHAT DO I CARE?

PEP RALLY!

I'VE BECOME **NEAT**, MY DEAR! NOTE THE NEW WARDROBE! NOT A WRINKLE OR CREASE ANYWHERE! I AM TO- TALLY PUT TOGETHER!

5/2

✳ SNORT! ✳.. PUT A BOW TIE ON A PIG, IT'S STILL A PIG.

FOR SOME REASON, SHE WENT OFF ON SOME IRRELEVANT TANGENT ABOUT FARM ANIMALS.

© 2007 by NEA, Inc.

WHAT'S UP, MR. CLEAN?

NOW THAT I'M NEAT, I... I DON'T THINK I CAN EAT MY LUNCH.

I MEAN, LOOK AT THESE CHEEZ DOODLES! LOOK HOW THE ORANGE POWDER GETS ALL OVER EVERYTHING!... IT'S **DISGUSTING!**

BUT YOU **LOVE** CHEEZ DOODLES!

I **KNOW**, BUT THEY... I **WANT** TO EAT THEM, BUT... THEY'RE TOO **MESSY!**

© 2007 by NEA, Inc.

ARE YOU CRYING, DUDE?

I'LL EAT THEM!

THIS IS A NIGHTMARE.

FRANCIS, I WANT YOU TO UN-HYPNOTIZE ME! I DON'T **LIKE** BEING NEAT!

I CAN'T **ENJOY** ANYTHING ANYMORE, BECAUSE ALL I CAN **THINK** ABOUT IS BEING **NEAT** AND **TIDY** ALL THE TIME!

BEING SO CLEAN MAKES ME FEEL... FEEL...

...DIRTY?

HOW IRONIC!

MAKE ME A SLOB AGAIN.

HERE'S MY HOME-WORK, MRS. G!

WHA-...? THIS IS A **MESS!**

WHAT HAPPENED TO THE **NEATNESS** OF THE PAST TWO WEEKS?

THAT'S OVER! I'M BACK TO MY OLD SELF!

5/12

BUT REST ASSURED: THE PAPER MAY LOOK A BIT SLOPPY ON THE **SURFACE**, BUT UNDERNEATH THE **QUALITY** OF MY WORK IS JUST THE SAME AS EVER!

© 2007 by NEA, Inc.

OH, GOODY.

OOP! ALMOST FORGOT! HERE'S PAGE TWO!

Peirce

NATE, I WANT YOU TO COVER TONIGHT'S SCHOOL BOARD MEETING FOR THE NEXT EDITION OF THE "WEEKLY BUGLE."

THE SCHOOL BOARD MEETING?

THEY'LL BE DISCUSSING NEXT YEAR'S BUDGET! IT'S AN IMPORTANT STORY!

GINA, THOSE MEETINGS ARE YAWN CITY!

WHY DO I HAVE TO COVER **THAT** STORY? WHY CAN'T I DO THE STORY IDEA **I** PROPOSED?

5/14

© 2007 by NEA, Inc.

"A SEARCH FOR THE SCHOOL'S MOST BOOTY-LICIOUS CHEER-LEADER"?

ONE REPORTER'S QUEST! UP CLOSE AND PERSONAL!

FIRST TIME AT A SCHOOL BOARD MEETING, AMIGO?

YUP

WELL, LET ME GIVE YOU THE LAY OF THE LAND, MY FRIEND! I'VE ATTENDED **MANY** OF THESE IN MY CAPACITY AS A FREE-LANCE PHOTOGRAPHER!

THE MOST IMPORTANT THING IS TO MAKE SURE YOU'RE PROP-ERLY **EQUIPPED!**

5/16

© 2007 by NEA, Inc.

WHAT'S IN THERE?

DOUGHNUTS, KID. THESE MEETINGS GIVE ME THE MUNCHIES.

Peirce

ARE YOU SUGGESTING SOME SORT OF **WAGER**?

MR. GALVIN, THIS WORK-SHEET ON PHOTOSYNTHESIS REALLY ISN'T WORKING FOR ME.

IT ISN'T "WORKING" FOR YOU?

WELL, LET ME EXPLAIN SOMETHING, NATE. THE WORKSHEET ISN'T "**WORKING**" FOR YOU BECAUSE IT'S A **PIECE** OF **PAPER**! IT'S NOT **SUPPOSED** TO "WORK"!

THE "WORK" PART IS WHERE **YOU** COME IN! **YOU** "WORK" ON THE "SHEET"! WHICH IS WHY IT'S CALLED A **WORK-SHEET**!

5/22

THAT DIDN'T WORK.

Peirce

OKAY, MR. GALVIN... **HERE'S** A JOKE I THINK YOU'LL APPRECIATE!

WHAT DID THE THEORETICAL PHYSICIST USE TO DRINK HIS BEER?

AN EINSTEIN!

WA HA HA HA HA HO HO HA

5/26

© 2007 by NEA, Inc.

WHAT KIND OF A SCIENCE TEACHER DOESN'T LAUGH AT A JOKE ABOUT THEORETICAL PHYSICS?

I'VE BEEN TRYING ALL **WEEK** TO GET MR. GALVIN TO LAUGH, BUT IT'S **IM-POSSIBLE!**

I'VE TOLD HIM EVERY JOKE I KNOW! EVERY RIDDLE!!

...BUT **NOTH-ING!**

I CAN GET HIM TO LAUGH!

YOU?? ☆ SNORT! ☆ **RIGHT,** GINA!

I'LL BET YOU FIVE BUCKS!

YOU'RE ON!

FOLLOW ME!

MR. GALVIN, NATE THINKS HE HAS A GOOD CHANCE TO MAKE THE HONOR ROLL THIS TERM. WHAT DO **YOU** THINK?

WELL, I... ☆ MMMPH! ☆

☆ AHEM! ☆ CHUCKLE!... HEH HEH...

WA HA HA HA HA HA HA HA

OH, THE INDIGNITY.

YOU KNOW, THAT WAS **WORTH** FIVE BUCKS!

MR. ROSA, WE'RE HAVING A MEETING OF THE CARTOONING CLUB AFTER SCHOOL TODAY!

THAT'S NICE.

SO... CAN YOU BE THERE?

ME?

IT'S A SCHOOL RULE THAT CLUBS NEED TO HAVE A TEACHER PRESENT AT MEETINGS, AND WE FIGURED YOU PROBABLY DON'T HAVE ANYTHING ELSE GOING ON!

SO SAD, BUT SO TRUE.

OH, AND CAN WE USE YOUR CLASS-ROOM?

© 2007 by NEA, Inc.

Peirce

WHEN DRAWING COMICS, CHAD, COMING UP WITH THE RIGHT SOUND EFFECT IS **CRUCIAL!**

ALMOST ANY SITUATION CAN BE MADE FUNNY BY THE ADDITION OF A HUMOROUS SOUND EFFECT!

KLONG!

PROPS ARE ALSO KEY!

OW!

YOU'RE **BOTH** RIGHT!

Peirce

WHEN DRAWING A COMIC STRIP, CHAD, YOU DON'T ALWAYS HAVE TO WAIT UNTIL THE FINAL PANEL TO DELIVER THE PUNCH LINE!

SOMETIMES YOU CAN PUT THE JOKE IN THE **NEXT-TO-LAST** PANEL! THEN THE **LAST** PANEL CAN BE JUST, YOU KNOW, A REACTION SHOT!

WOO WOO WOO WOO WOO

BOING! BOING!

NOW, WHERE WAS I?

Peirce

67

WHATCHA READING THERE, MRS. CZERWICKI?

ER... WELL...

"PYRAMIDS OF PASSION"! OOOH! LET'S TAKE A LOOK AT THE BACK COVER, SHALL WE?

ZIP!

"WHILE EXCAVATING THE TOMB OF HAKHOTAN, SHAPELY SCIENTIST MAURA ALBRIGHT FINDS HERSELF ENCHANTED BY THE RUGGED EGYPTOLOGIST ADAM CASSEL, BEHIND WHOSE ICY BLUE EYES BURNS A FIRE HOTTER THAN THE DESERT SUN."

6/5

MRS. CZER-WICKI! ROWR!

I'VE... ✕AHEM!✕ ALWAYS BEEN INTERESTED IN ARCHAEOLOGY.

peirce

FIRST TIME, KID?

YES. ARE THEY GOING TO CALL MY PARENTS?

YUP. THEY ALWAYS CALL YOUR PARENTS WHEN YOU GET DETENTION.

OHHH... THEY'RE GOING TO BE SO MAD.

KID, RELAX. MY DAD WAS UPSET THE FIRST COUPLE TIMES, BUT AFTER A FEW DOZEN, HE GOT USED TO IT.

6/7

© 2007 by NEA, Inc.

A FEW DOZEN?

WHEN I HIT TRIPLE DIGITS, HE JUST BECAME NUMB.

Peirce

YOU MAY BE HAPPY GETTING DETENTION EVERY DAY, BUT NOT **ME!**

ONCE IS ENOUGH! I'VE LEARNED MY LESSON! I'M NEVER GOING TO GET DE-TENTION **AGAIN!**

$\frac{6}{9}$

I'M GOING TO TURN MY LIFE AROUND! I'M GOING TO BE THE TYPE OF STUDENT THIS SCHOOL CAN BE **PROUD** OF!

© 2007 by NEA, Inc.

WHAT A LOSER.

Peirce

SIR? I HAVE A NOTE FOR YOU FROM NATE WRIGHT.

FROM NATE WRIGHT?

HE DROPPED IT OFF ON HIS WAY TO CLASS.

ALL RIGHT THEN. THANK YOU, MRS. SHIPULSKI.

Dear Principal Nichols,

Hi there, big guy. I hope your morning is going OK so far.

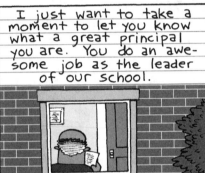

I just want to take a moment to let you know what a great principal you are. You do an awesome job as the leader of our school.

You inspire confidence and make us feel safe. And speaking of safety, I couldn't help noticing we haven't had a fire drill recently.

So, could we have a fire drill this morning? And could it happen at precisely 9:30?

Thanks! Sincerely,

Nate Wright

CLUNK!

YOU HAVE FORTY MINUTES TO COMPLETE THIS TEST. BEGIN.

I SHOULD HAVE INCLUDED A BRIBE.

MRS. GODFREY, SINCE THE WEATHER IS SO NICE, CAN WE HAVE CLASS OUTSIDE? PLEEEZ?

NO.

BUT MR. ROSA LET US HAVE **ART** OUTSIDE, AND IT WAS **AWESOME!**

I'M NOT MR. ROSA.

SHE'S NOT MR. ROSA.

NEWS FLASH.

© 2007 by NEA, Inc.

MS. CLARKE, CAN WE HAVE CLASS OUTSIDE?

OUT- SIDE?

MR. ROSA SAID YES. MRS. GODFREY AND MR. GALVIN SAID NO.

6/15

ARE YOU GOING TO ALLY YOUR- SELF WITH ROSA, OR WITH GODFREY AND GALVIN?

WELL PLAYED.

I UNDER- STAND FACULTY DYNAMICS.

MR. STAPLES, IT'S SUCH A NICE DAY THAT WE'VE BEEN ASKING TEACHERS TO LET US HAVE CLASS OUTSIDE.

TWO TEACHERS HAVE SAID **YES**, TWO HAVE SAID **NO**. WE HAVE A **TIE**, AND ONLY **YOU** CAN BREAK IT!

THE CLOCK IS TICKING, MR. STAPLES.

IT'S HERO TIME.

SCORE! I HAPPEN TO KNOW THE MAN PLAYED DIVISION 3 BASKETBALL!

CHECK THIS OUT.

HEY NATE: WHO WAS THE MVP OF SUPER BOWL XV?

JIM PLUNKETT.

WHAT TEACHER DOES LINUS HAVE A CRUSH ON IN "PEANUTS"?

MISS OTHMAR.

WHAT'S JACKIE CHAN'S REAL NAME?

CHAN KONG-SANG.

WHAT YEAR WAS ZZ TOP INDUCTED INTO THE ROCK AND ROLL HALL OF FAME?

2004.

WHO DIRECTED "NACHO LIBRE"?

JARED HESS.

WHAT'S TWELVE TIMES SEVEN?

UHHH...

WAIT. LET ME THINK.

FASCINATING.

IT ALSO WORKS WITH STATE CAPITALS.

© 2007 by NEA, Inc.

ALL RIGHT, PEOPLE, SETTLE DOWN! THERE WILL BE NO "PRANK DAY" SHENANIGANS IN **THIS** ROOM!

6/20

WE STILL HAVE ONE FINAL CLASS TO GET THROUGH, AND...

DELIVERY.

WHAT?

THE "THIGHMASTER" YOU ORDERED, MA'AM.

© 2007 by NEA, Inc.

HA HA HA HA HA HA HA HA HA HA HA

CRIPES.

HI, KIDS.

HA HA HA HA HA

Peirce

© 2007 by NEA, Inc.

AHH, **SUMMER!**

NO SCHOOL TO THINK ABOUT! NO TEACHERS TO BOSS US AROUND! WE'RE **FREE!**

WE CAN DO ANYTHING WE WANT! THE POSSIBILITIES ARE ENDLESS! IT'S A BIG WORLD OUT THERE!

! MR. GALVIN!

YOU'RE JAYWALKING, BOYS. USE THE CROSS-WALK.

FIND SOMEWHERE ELSE TO PLAY FRISBEE, BOYS. YOU MIGHT HIT SOMEONE.

PRINCIPAL NICHOLS!

HOW'S THAT OFF-SEASON CONDITIONING PROGRAM GOING, LADIES?

COACH JOHN!

IF YOU WANT TO HAVE A **PRAYER** OF COMPLETING THE SUMMER READING LIST, I SUGGEST YOU HEAD FOR THE LIBRARY.

! !

IT MIGHT BE A BIG WORLD, BUT IT'S A SMALL, SMALL TOWN.

I CAN'T WAIT TO GO OFF TO COLLEGE.

IT'S 12:30! IF WE WERE IN SCHOOL RIGHT NOW, WE'D BE SITTING IN MRS. GODFREY'S CLASS LISTENING TO HER YAMMERING ABOUT... ABOUT...

...HEY, WHAT'S THE NAME OF THAT GUY SHE TOLD US ABOUT LAST WEEK?

WHO **CARES**? WHY EVEN **THINK** ABOUT IT?

6/29

YEAH, BUT NOW THAT I CAN'T THINK OF IT, IT'S DRIVING ME CRAZY.

QUIT THINKING ABOUT IT! IT'S **SUMMER**! DON'T **RUIN** IT!

© 2007 by NEA, Inc.

MA'AM? WHO WAS THE GUY WHO RAN FOR PRESIDENT AGAINST ABE LINCOLN AND THEN ENDED UP AS THE SECRETARY OF....

YOU'RE **RUIN-ING IT!!**

WHAT'S WITH THE STICK?

JUST MAKING A POINT, TEDDY.

I KEEP TELLING COACH THAT NOTHING EVER HAPPENS OUT HERE IN RIGHT FIELD!

TO PROVE MY POINT, I'M MARK-ING THIS SPOT!

...AND I'LL BET I WON'T HAVE TO MOVE FROM THIS SPOT FOR THE WHOLE GAME!

CRACK!

WELL! LOOKS LIKE I **WILL** HAVE TO MOVE!

OOP! IT'S NOT CARRYING LIKE I THOUGHT IT WOULD!

ARRGH! NOW THE **WIND'S** TAKING IT!

THE SUN'S IN MY EYES! WHERE **IS** IT?

THERE IT IS!

N A B!

I LOVE GOLF, BUT I'VE NEVER REALLY PLAYED A ROUND THAT **MEANS** ANYTHING!

I'D LOVE TO KNOW WHAT IT WOULD FEEL LIKE TO BE A PRO! TO PLAY FOR **HIGH STAKES!**

I'D LOVE TO FIND OUT HOW I'D REACT UNDER **PRESSURE!**

YOU WANT PRESSURE?

YOU'RE DOWN TO YOUR LAST BALL, AND WE'RE ONLY ON THE TWELFTH HOLE.

YIKES.

"POOR NATE'S ALMANAC"? WHAT'S THIS?

I'M FOLLOWING IN THE FOOTSTEPS OF BEN FRANKLIN, BOYS!

POOR NATE'S ALMANAC $2

BACK IN THE 1700s, OL' BEN PUBLISHED "POOR RICHARD'S ALMANACK"!

IT WAS FILLED WITH ALL SORTS OF WISE SAYINGS LIKE "THE EARLY BIRD GETS THE WORM" AND "A PENNY SAVED IS A PENNY EARNED"!

"POOR NATE'S ALMANAC" IS THE SAME THING, ONLY **BETTER!** YOU WON'T BELIEVE ALL THE WISDOM IN HERE!

POOR NATE'S

AND THESE ARE MY LAST TWO COPIES! A BARGAIN AT TWO BUCKS EACH!

OKAY, I'LL TAKE ONE.

ME TOO!

HEY! THIS THING'S **BLANK!**

WAIT, THERE'S SOMETHING WRITTEN ON THE LAST PAGE.

FLIP FLIP FLIP

There's a sucker born every minute.

I DON'T WANT TO RAIN ON YOUR PARADE, DAD, BUT DO YOU REALLY THINK YOU CAN RUN A 10K?

WHY NOT?

IT'S OVER SIX MILES!

SO? LOOK, I ALREADY DO A DAILY LAP AROUND THE BLOCK!

7/10

TO TRAIN FOR THE RACE, ALL I NEED TO DO IS INCREASE THAT BY A LAP OR TWO!

...OR TWENTY-FOUR.

TWENTY-FOUR?

AND SPEAKING OF TRAINING... MIGHT BE A GOOD IDEA TO LOSE THE DOUGHNUT.

Peirce

DAD, IF YOU'RE GONNA RUN A 10K, YOU SHOULD LET ME BE YOUR TRAINER.

WHY'S THAT?

BECAUSE I KNOW WHAT I'M DOING! REMEMBER, I HAD TO RUN A 5-MILER TO GET MY PHYSICAL FITNESS MERIT BADGE!

THERE'S STUFF YOU NEED TO KNOW, DAD! THERE ARE "DOS" AND "DON'TS" IN THE WORLD OF RUNNING!

THE SOCKS, FOR INSTANCE, ARE A "DON'T."

THEY ARE?

© 2007 by NEA, Inc.

AARRGH!

WHAT HAPPENED? DID I JERK MY HEAD UP?

NOPE

DID I ROLL MY WRISTS?

NOPE

WAS I PAST HORIZONTAL ON MY BACKSWING?

NO

DID MY FRONT HIP FLY OPEN?

NO

DID I TURN MY SHOULDERS TOO EARLY?

NOPE

I DON'T GET IT. WHAT DID I DO WRONG?

WHAT DID I DO WRONG?

YOU HIT YOUR BALL INTO THE WOODS.

WRONG ANSWER.

KEEP LOOKING.

MAN, I'M SO BROKE.

ME TOO.

YOU KNOW WHAT WE SHOULD DO? GO TO A **YARD SALE**!

WE TAKE THE LITTLE BIT OF CASH WE HAVE, SEE, AND WE BUY SOMETHING! SOMETHING THAT **LOOKS** LIKE A WORTHLESS PIECE OF **JUNK**!

7/16

...BUT THEN WE TAKE IT ON "ANTIQUES ROADSHOW" AND FIND OUT IT'S ACTUALLY WORTH A **FORTUNE**!

AND THEN WE'LL HAVE ENOUGH MONEY TO GO SEE "EVAN ALMIGHTY"?

RIGHT! WITH UN-LIMITED "JUNIOR MINTS"!

GUYS, HELP ME PEEK BEHIND THE BACK OF THIS PAINTING!

WHAT FOR?

HAVEN'T YOU HEARD ABOUT THAT GUY WHO BOUGHT AN OLD PAINTING AT A YARD SALE?

LATER, WHEN HE TOOK OFF THE BACKING, HE FOUND A COPY OF THE **DECLARATION OF INDEPENDENCE!**

7/19

© 2007 by NEA, Inc.

DUDE, THIS IS A VELVET SILKSCREEN OF DOGS PLAYING POKER.

EXACTLY! WHERE BETTER TO HIDE VALUABLES? BEHIND A **CLASSIC!**

AHEM! UH... HOW MUCH FOR THIS JUNKY OL' PICTURE?

HM?...TEN CENTS.

SOLD! HA! MY GOOD MAN, YOU MAY HAVE JUST MADE ME **RICH**!

THIS PICTURE YOU JUST SOLD ME FOR A **DIME** LOOKS TO BE AN AUTHENTIC PHOTOGRAPH OF A YOUNG **ABE LINCOLN**!

7/20

KID, THAT'S A POSTCARD OF KEANU REEVES THAT MY DAUGHTER DREW A BEARD ON WITH A "SHARPIE".

IT IS?

SMOOTH MOVE, EX-LAX.

THREE MORE, AND YOU'LL BREAK YOUR ALL-TIME RECORD!

NO PROBLEM!

SWISH!

TWO MORE! THAT'S PRESSURE SHOOTING!

"PRESSURE"? WHAT IS THIS "PRESSURE" YOU SPEAK OF?

SWISH!

I DON'T EVEN KNOW THE **MEANING** OF PRESSURE!

HELLO, BOYS.

MRS. GODFREY!

ULP!

I'M ON MY WAY OVER TO A READING AT THAT NEW BOOKSTORE!

HM.

UH HUH

OH, BUT I DIDN'T MEAN TO INTERRUPT YOU! KEEP SHOOTING, NATE!

UH... OKAY.

CLANG!

TSK! SO CLOSE!

NOW DO YOU KNOW THE MEANING OF PRESSURE?

OH, HOW I HATE HER.

THESE GUYS ARE PRETTY COCKY, CHESTER! HOW ABOUT SHUTTING THEM UP BY PITCHING A NO-HITTER?

CHESTER?

I'M TRYING TO DO MY PRE-GAME ROUTINE.

I'M TRYING TO GO TO MY HAPPY PLACE. I DON'T LIKE PEOPLE BOTHERING ME WHEN I'M IN MY HAPPY PLACE.

7/25

HEAR THAT, FELLAS? BACK OFF!

GET OUT OF MY HAPPY PLACE OR I'LL RIP YOUR ARM OFF.

Peirce

I STILL CAN'T BELIEVE THE OTHER TEAM HAD A **SCOUTING REPORT** ON ME!

SO YOU KEEP SAYING.

Y'KNOW, IT WOULDN'T SURPRISE ME IF SOME **PRO** SCOUTS HAVE THEIR EYES ON ME!

PRO SCOUTS? YOU'RE **ELEVEN YEARS OLD!**

SO? TAKE A LOOK AT THAT GUY UP THERE! HAVE YOU NOTICED HE'S AT ALL OUR GAMES? HAVE YOU SEEN THE WAY HE'S ALWAYS WRITING ON THAT NOTEPAD?

$\frac{7}{28}$

DUDE, THAT'S MY UNCLE PEDRO.

OH.

AND I THINK HE'S DO-ING AN "ACROSTIC."

FRANCIS! DO YOU BELIEVE IN OMENS?

I GUESS SO.

WELL, IF I MAKE THIS SHOT, IT'S AN OMEN THAT I'M GOING TO BE RICH!

IF I MAKE IT WITHOUT HITTING THE BACKBOARD, IT MEANS I'M GOING TO BE FAMOUS!

...AND IF I MAKE IT WITHOUT HITTING THE BACKBOARD **OR** THE RIM, IT MEANS I'M GOING TO MARRY A SUPER-MODEL!

FLing!

CLANG!

CRASH!

MYOWR!

Screeee.. THUMP!

WHAT IF YOU MISS, AND THEN THE BALL BREAKS A WINDOW, HITS A CAT, ROLLS INTO THE STREET, AND GETS RUN OVER BY A DUMP TRUCK?

THEN IT'S A PRACTICE SHOT.

LOOK AT THAT TECHNIQUE! RUSTY SIENNA IS THE GREATEST PAINTER IN THE WORLD TODAY!

THEN WHAT'S HE DOING HOSTING A CHEESY TV SHOW? WHY ISN'T HE IN A MUSEUM OR SOMETHING?

LOOK, TEDDY, DON'T ASK ME TO EXPLAIN THE ABSURDITIES OF THE ART WORLD!

ALL I KNOW IS: WHEN RUSTY PAINTS A LAKE, IT LOOKS LIKE A LAKE! WHEN HE PAINTS A TREE, IT LOOKS LIKE A TREE! WHEN HE PAINTS AN ALP, IT LOOKS LIKE AN ALP!

7/31

"AN ALP"?

YOU CAN TELL IT'S AN ALP BECAUSE OF THE SHEPHERD GIRL IN THE CORNER.

© 2007 by NEA, Inc.

WHAT'S UP?

I JUST GOOGLED RUSTY SIENNA! I'M THINKING OF SENDING HIM A FAN LETTER!

LET'S SEE... "RUSTY SIENNA, AMERICA'S FAVORITE TELEVISION ARTIST... BLAH BLAH BLAH... BORN APRIL 28TH, 1940.".

8/2

"DIED MAY 7TH, 1996."

© 2007 by NEA, Inc.

WHAT?!

YOU KNOW, I **THOUGHT** HE LOOKED KIND OF PALE.

Peirce

WHAT THE...? RUSTY SIENNA IS **DEAD**? HE'S **DEAD**?

YUP, ACCORDING TO THIS WEB SITE.

BUT!... THE GUY'S ON TV **EVERY DAY**!

UH, HEL**LO**? EVER HEAR OF **RERUNS**?

SO... ALL THOSE PAINTINGS HE DOES... THOSE ARE **RERUNS**? THOSE ARE, LIKE... TWENTY YEARS OLD?

GUESS SO.

8/3

BUT... THEY SEEM SO FRESH AND CONTEMPORARY!

YES, THEY DO HAVE THAT QUALITY.

Peirce

I CAN'T **BELIEVE** THIS NEWS ABOUT RUSTY SIENNA! I'M IN **SHOCK!**

IT SAYS HERE HE DIED WHILE TAPING HIS TV SHOW, "OIL PAINTING WITH RUSTY," BACK IN 1996.

SO THE MAN I'VE IDOLIZED FOR MY WHOLE LIFE HAS BEEN SECRETLY **DEAD** THE ENTIRE TIME?

"SECRETLY DEAD"?

ACTUALLY, LET'S NOT THINK OF HIM AS "DEAD." LET'S THINK OF HIM AS "TIMELESS."

HERE YA GO, KID.

THANKS!

SLUP!

NO, SPITSY! BACK OFF! THIS IS **MINE**!

WURF!

I SAID **NO**, YOU FLEABAG! I'M **NOT** SHARING MY ICE CREAM!

AND DON'T ASK ME TO BUY YOU ONE OF YOUR **OWN**, EITHER! I'M OUT OF MONEY!

WOORF?

WHIMPER...

❊ SIGH... ❊

ALL RIGHT, ALL RIGHT... GIVE ME THAT TENNIS BALL.

FRANCIS.

HM?

CATCH.

GAH!

DON'T SAY I NEVER DO ANYTHING NICE FOR YOU.

SLORPF
SLORPF
SLORPF
SLORPF
SLORPF

DAD, LET ME GIVE IT TO YOU STRAIGHT: I'M NOT SURE YOU'RE READY TO RUN A 10K.

OH, COME ON, NATE!

YOU ACT AS IF I'M TOTALLY INEXPERIENCED! I'LL HAVE YOU KNOW THAT I WAS A MEMBER OF MY HIGH SCHOOL TRACK TEAM!

YEAH, I KNEW THAT.

YOU DID?

I'VE SEEN YOUR YEARBOOK.

YOU HAVE?

8/7

HE WAS THE EQUIPMENT MANAGER.

BUSTED.

© 2007 by NEA, Inc.

WHAT ARE YOU DOING?

PRINTING A MAP OF YOUR RACE ROUTE.

WHIRRRR

YOU START AT THE HIGH SCHOOL, AND THE FINISH LINE IS NEAR THE GOLF COURSE.

WAIT, WAIT A MINUTE... WAY OUT **THERE**?

THAT... WOW!... THAT SEEMS LONGER THAN... I MEAN... I'VE DRIVEN THAT ROUTE AND IT'S PRETTY... UH... HOW FAR **IS** THAT, EXACTLY?

EXACTLY TEN KILOMETERS, DAD.

ARE THEY **SURE**? I MEAN, HAVE THEY MEASURED IT?

$\frac{8}{10}$ Peirce

ARRGH!

WHAT'S UP, DAD?

I'VE BEEN TRYING TO FIGURE OUT THIS BRAIN TEASER FOR AN **HOUR**!

MAY I?

BE MY GUEST. IT'S **IMPOSSIBLE**!

MM.... MMM HMM...

GOT IT. THE SISTERS WERE BORN IN THIS ORDER: ELEANOR, EILEEN, ELIZABETH, EMILY AND EVELYN.

THAT WAS THE EASIEST BRAIN TEASER I'VE EVER SEEN.

THE PROBLEM WITH TEASING IS THAT IT OFTEN LEADS TO OUTRIGHT HUMILIATION.

Peirce

WANT TO KNOW, ONCE AND FOR ALL, WHY CATS ARE BETTER THAN DOGS?

NOT REALLY.

THEY'RE MORE **AGILE!** COMPARED TO CATS, DOGS ARE SLOW AND CLUMSY!

HERE'S AN EXAMPLE: IF YOU DROPPED A CAT UPSIDE DOWN FROM A SECOND-FLOOR WINDOW, WHAT WOULD HAPPEN?

IT WOULD LAND ON ITS **FEET!**

NOW!... WHAT WOULD HAPPEN IF YOU DROPPED A **DOG** UPSIDE DOWN FROM THAT VERY SAME SECOND-FLOOR WINDOW?

IT WOULD LAND ON THE CAT.

HIGH FIVE!

THAT'S WHY YOU DROP THE CAT FIRST!

WHERE **IS** IT? I REMEMBER BURYING MY TIME CAPSULE **RIGHT HERE!**

MAYBE YOUR MEMORY IS WRONG.

MY MEMORY IS **PERFECT!** I REMEMBER DIGGING FOR HOURS IN THE BLAZING SUN, AND IT WAS ALL DUSTY, AND I FOUND THIS LITTLE THING WITH INITIALS ON IT, AND...

8/21

DUDE, THAT WAS "HOLES". WE WATCHED IT AT MY HOUSE LAST WEEK.

© 2007 by NEA, Inc.

WELL, THAT WOULD EXPLAIN THE PRESENCE OF JON VOIGHT.

HE'S EASILY CONFUSED.

I'M HEADING HOME.

WHAT? FRANCIS, WE HAVEN'T FINISHED LOOKING AT ALL THE STUFF IN MY TIME CAPSULE!

THOSE THINGS ARE ONLY THREE YEARS OLD! THEY HAVE NO HISTORICAL VALUE!

NO HISTORICAL VALUE? NO HISTORICAL VALUE?

WHAT ABOUT "FEMME FATALITY" # 64, WHERE SHE BATTLES THE MOLE PEOPLE OF VENTRIS-3?

FEMME FATAL

8/25

AS I SAID...

BUT THIS IS THE VERY FIRST ISSUE TO FEATURE HER LEOPARD-SKIN TUBE TOP!

Peirce

153

© 2007 by NEA, Inc.

8/28

155

GAAH!

WHAT IS IT, NATE?

OH, MAN! WHAT A **HORRIBLE** NIGHTMARE!

MRS. **GODFREY** WAS IN IT!... AND SHE WAS **LIVING** HERE IN OUR **HOUSE**, AND...

EASY, SON. YOU'RE STRESSED ABOUT SCHOOL STARTING UP AGAIN, THAT'S ALL.

TELL YOU WHAT: JUST RELAX, AND I'LL BRING YOU A MUG OF HOT COCOA!

OKAY. THANKS, DAD.

WE'RE OUT OF COCOA...

GAAH!

HOW ABOUT A NICE TALL GLASS OF ASPARAGUS JUICE?

The Monday known as Labor Day
Is cause for celebration;
A tribute to the efforts of
All those who've built this nation.

How is this day devoted to
The "Working Man" observed?
We leave our jobs behind and take
A rest most well-deserved.

I say to you: enjoy yourself!
And seize the day, my friend.
For when tomorrow rolls around...

...The grind begins again.

Public School 38

WELCOME BACK
STUDENTS

© 2007 by NEA, Inc.

172

BOYS, ONE OF OUR PROBLEMS LAST YEAR, FRANKLY, WAS OUR **CONDITIONING!**

WE JUST SEEMED TO RUN OUT OF GAS AT THE END OF GAMES! WE WANT TO AVOID THAT **THIS** YEAR!

...SO I'M BRINGING IN A **SPECIALIST** TO HELP YOU GENTS WITH YOUR STAMINA! **COACH JOHN!**

ACTUALLY, I WAS PERFECTLY CONTENT WITH RUNNING OUT OF GAS AT THE END OF GAMES.

TEA PARTY'S OVER, LADIES!

SO! THE TASK AT HAND, AS I UNDERSTAND IT, IS TO WHIP YOU MARSHMALLOWS INTO **SHAPE**!

THAT'LL TAKE **WORK**, SOLDIERS! **LOTS** OF WORK! BUT JUST REMEMBER **THIS**:

"THAT WHICH DOES NOT **KILL** ME MAKES ME **STRONGER**"!!

9/18

© 2007 by NEA, Inc.

SO HE'S ONLY GOING TO **ALMOST** KILL US?

GULP!

FIRST RULE: IF YOU'RE GOING TO TOSS YOUR COOKIES, DO IT ON THE **SIDE-LINES**!

Peirce

HANG IN THERE, GUYS! I KNOW COACH JOHN IS A BIT OF A TASK-MASTER, BUT HAVING HIM HELP OUT WILL PAY BIG DIVIDENDS!

COACH

GASP! WHEW!

DID I EVER TELL YOU HE WAS **MY** COACH BACK IN HIGH SCHOOL? HE WAS HIRED RIGHT BEFORE MY SENIOR YEAR, AND WHAT A YEAR THAT WAS!

COAC

INSTEAD OF LOSING ALL **TEN** OF OUR GAMES, WE ONLY LOST **NINE**!

COAC

THAT'S LAME-TASTIC!

OUR WIN WAS A FORFEIT, BUT WE FELT **GOOD** ABOUT OURSELVES!

9/22

Peirce

180

NOW THAT WE'RE A BAND, WHAT SHOULD WE DO FIRST?

LET'S THINK UP A NAME!

HOLD ON, LADS.

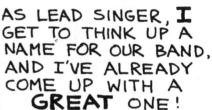

AS LEAD SINGER, **I** GET TO THINK UP A NAME FOR OUR BAND, AND I'VE ALREADY COME UP WITH A **GREAT** ONE!

ENSLAVE THE MOLLUSK!

"ENSLAVE THE MOLLUSK"?

HOW COME **YOU** GET TO BE THE LEAD SINGER?

I'VE GOT THE BEST HAIR.

PRETTY COOL, EH GUYS? MY DAD SAID WE COULD USE THE GARAGE FOR BAND PRACTICE!

SOON THE NEIGHBORHOOD WILL BE FILLED WITH THE SOUNDS OF "ENSLAVE THE MOLLUSK" PLAYING HEAD-BANGING, EARTH-SHATTERING **ROCK!**

WHO BROUGHT SOME MUSIC?

I DID! TWO SONGS!

MY "HOT CROSS BUNS" IS PRETTY GOOD, BUT MY "BAA BAA BLACK SHEEP" NEEDS A LITTLE WORK.

THAT'S GOOD TO KNOW.

I BORROWED MY UNCLE'S GUITAR, AND HE SHOWED ME A FEW "POWER CHORDS"!

IT'S BEEN A YEAR SINCE I QUIT PIANO LESSONS, BUT I CAN STILL PLAY HALF-DECENT KEYBOARDS!

...AND **I'M** THE MAN ON THE MICROPHONE! THIS IS **AWESOME**, YOU GUYS! WE'RE A REAL LIVE **BAND!**

FOR THOSE ABOUT TO ROCK!... WE SALUUUUTE YOUUU!

© 2007 by NEA, Inc.

PERHAPS WE CAN SPECIALIZE IN INSTRUMENTALS.

I WAS JUST THINKING THAT.

10/5

© 2007 by NEA, Inc.

YOU'RE THE NICKNAME CZAR, RIGHT? I HAVE A NEW NICKNAME FOR MRS. GODFREY!

LET'S HEAR IT.

"CRUELLA"! 'CAUSE, YOU KNOW, SHE'S SO MEAN!

HM. NOPE. SORRY, GUY.

THAT'S TOO STRAIGHT-FORWARD! A GOOD NICKNAME WORKS ON **MANY** LEVELS!

TAKE ONE OF MY FAVORITE NAMES FOR MRS. GODFREY: "DARK SIDE OF THE MOON"!

THE "DARK SIDE" OBVIOUSLY, REFERS TO MRS. GODFREY'S SOUL. SHE HAS TURNED TO THE DARK SIDE AND EMBRACED EVIL AS A WAY OF LIFE.

THE MOON, LIKE MRS. GODFREY, IS HUGE, INHOSPITABLE AND DEVOID OF BEAUTY.

AND FINALLY, THE MOON'S DARK SIDE IS EXTREMELY COLD — EXACTLY LIKE MRS. GODFREY, WHO HAS NO WARMTH OR KINDNESS.

KEEP TRYING, KID.

THE GREAT ONES MAKE IT LOOK SO EASY.

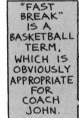

WHA...? WHY ARE THEY PLAYING **THIS** SONG ON "OLDIES 98.9"?

BECAUSE IT'S AN OLDIE, I GUESS.

BUT THIS SONG CAME OUT IN, LIKE, **1982**! 1982 IS NOT THAT LONG AGO!

ONLY A QUARTER CENTURY.

CRUNCH!

10/15

© 2007 by NEA, Inc.

DAD?

I JUST NEED TO LIE DOWN FOR A MINUTE.

HELLO, "OLDIES 98.9"? WHAT'S UP WITH YOU GUYS? YOU USED TO PLAY STUFF FROM THE SIXTIES AND SEVENTIES!

NOW YOU'RE PLAYING **CYNDI LAUPER** SONGS! CYNDI LAUPER IS **NOT** AN **OLDIE**!

UH... NO, I HAVEN'T SEEN HER LATELY.

THEY'VE GOT A POINT THERE.

HI, "OLDIES 98.9"?
CAN YOU PLAY "LITTLE
BITTY PRETTY ONE" BY
THURSTON HARRIS?
WHAT?... WHY NOT?

YES, I **KNOW** YOU'VE
CHANGED YOUR FORMAT,
BUT... WHAT?... WELL,
YOU'RE STILL CALLING
YOURSELF AN OLDIES
STATION! WHY CAN'T
I REQUEST AN OLDIE?

WHAT DO YOU MEAN,
"THAT'S **TOO** OLD"?
LISTEN, YOU CAN'T...
WHAT?... WHAT DOES
IT MATTER HOW OLD
I AM? LET ME
TELL YOU SOMETHING,
SONNY, I'M
NOT... HELLO?
HELLO?

10
18

I NEVER KNEW
EXACTLY WHAT THE
PHRASE "MIDLIFE
CRISIS" MEANT UNTIL
JUST NOW.

GUYS, HELP ME PICK OUT A GOOD MIDDLE NAME!

I'VE NARROWED IT DOWN TO CAESAR, SOLOMON, ARTHUR, ALEXANDER...

...AUGUSTUS, ZEUS, CONSTANTINE, HENRY, CHARLEMAGNE, AND JUSTINIAN!

10 26

© 2007 by NEA, Inc.

I'M DETECTING A THEME.

EVER HEARD THE PHRASE, "NAPOLEON COMPLEX"?

OOH, NAPOLEON! THAT'S A GOOD ONE!

© 2007 by NEA, Inc.

DAD, HAVE YOU EVER THOUGHT ABOUT HOW THIS AFFECTS **ME?**

HOW WHAT AFFECTS YOU?

THE WHOLE HALLOWEEN THING! EVERYBODY KNOWS THAT **MY DAD** IS THE NIMROD WHO HANDS OUT **PRUNES** TO TRICK-OR-TREATERS!

DO YOU HAVE ANY IDEA HOW EMBARRASSING THAT IS FOR ME?

11
2

© 2007 by NEA, Inc.

DID YOU JUST CALL ME A NIMROD?

FIRE UP THE **SHAME-CAM,** FOLKS! I'M READY FOR MY **CLOSE-UP!**

Peirce